This Notebook Belongs To:

If Found, Please Contact Me At:

Be Fierce.
Be Authentic.
Be Badass.

Your guide to thrive
instead of survive during
BIG life changes using the
FAB approach

Jennifer Day

Fantabulous Legal Disclaimer

Be **F**ierce.
Be **A**uthentic.
Be **B**adass.
Your guide to thrive instead of survive during
BIG life changes using the **FAB** approach
is a work of my own creation.

The information in this book was correct at the time of
publication, and the Author does not assume any liability for
loss or damage caused by errors or omissions, again, this is
my perspective, opinion, and experience, so it has been
written as such.

ISBN - 978-1-961185-55-5

www.inomniaparatuspublishing.com

Foreward

This isn't your everyday journal. This is a transformational experience created just for YOU as a simple, easy guide to the FAB Approach. You get to decide how deep you're willing to go as it's truly about the inner work we do that brings happiness and fulfillment to the surface.

Set aside some YOU time. Maybe that is 15-30 minutes, an hour, or a rainy afternoon. Take some time to think about what IS working in your life. Make a list. Write it down so you can refer to it when you having moments of frustration. Remind yourself that "you don't know what you don't know yet". Let that be enough in time of stress, anxiety, and simply breathe.

Now ask yourself what ISN'T working or what could use additional work. Make a list of that as well. Do not hold any judgment about this list, just write it all down. This is information you will use later.

You are intuitive and so is your body. If you don't necessarily hear or feel it talking to you lately, rest assured that you will gain some skills to be able to hear it again. It will take some practice connecting your mind with your body. As you lean in, you will begin to see the subtle ways your body tells you when it needs you to pay attention to its cues.

Think about what YOU want in life. There are prompts and quotes to get you thinking about ways to create the path to get there. I'm here to guide you each step of the way.

When we deny our stories, they define us. When we own our stories, we get to write a brave new ending."
~ Brené Brown, The Power of Vulnerability TED Talk

You are Fierce.
You are Authentic.
You are a Badass.

And I can't wait to hear about how
you healed to get there!

XO, Jenn

Do you find yourself here wondering what is next in for you and your life? How did you start out in one place and end up where you are now?
Ask yourself where did the parts of me that made me feel fearless, in charge, or badass disappear to?

If the answer is yes to one or more, you are in the right place! This has transformational journal prompts and quotes meant to generate thought-provoking perspectives of your life.
(I may be a little obsessed with Brené Brown quotes, lol)

You are the creator of your story (not your parents, grandparents, teachers, friends, or anyone who thinks they know best for you), just imperfectly perfect you.

You can stay on the surface level with your thoughts; however, I'd encourage you to dive deep into the workings of what makes you tick with these prompts. Remember to sit and think about each one and how the quotes tie together.

If you find yourself getting bored or zoning out, make a note of it as you have reached an edge of your comfort zone for that particular topic and use the empty left-hand pages to doodle & lighten up your energy.

Introduction

Healer

I am Fierce (in the best way).
How often do you celebrate what is working in life? Gratitude each day for even the smallest of things brings more of what we want. What isn't working? Acknowledgement brings the opportunity to find clarity, healing and be happy.

Change Management

I am Authentic.
After becoming burnt out in a stressful corporate job, I started learning about what made me tick. I began making healthy changes in my surroundings (including people, foods, activities, and movement). I want this for you as well.

Empowerment Coach

I am Badass.
People are meant to be in community, to feel seen and heard and enjoy life. There needs to be a safe place for this connection to happen. I provide that space for you to dive in and learn to thrive!

The inner work still needed on the left, became the ongoing result on the right through healing.

June 2017

Sept 2023

I am Intuitive.
As a kid, I didn't know that my ability to feel others energy was going to be helpful as an adult. Once I started connecting with like-minded people and learning my Human Design, making BIG life changes has become easier. I can't wait for you to EMBRACE big change too!

I am a Healer.
I have been given many tough situations in life to build my capacity and resilience to overcome challenges. I am a cancer survivor. I've lost 125 physical pounds, PLUS an enormous amount emotional weight.

It became clear that in overcoming these challenges, I was meant to help you with your mind-body connection and healing as well.

LET'S CONNECT

In becoming my authentic self, I resisted, was challenged,
poked, and prodded in all the energetic ways to realize
that I could have better because I deserved better!
Guess what?
You are here because the Universe brought us together.

Now that you know a bit about me,
I want to know who YOU are!
Connect with me through my FREE Facebook community

facebook.com/groups/fabapproachcommunity

scan to connect

Highly recommend Jen, although I have known her personally for many years I've recently worked with her in a professional capacity. I have done countless therapies since the death of my son by suicide in 2018. This was different although very therapeutic it takes away that constant depth of reliving trauma experiences and replaces it with avenues to casually talk about it. Jen is a compassionate person in general and has a way to relate even though her experiences have been different and bring a simpler approach to understanding the need for self care, communication and understanding those dreaded feelings. I encourage anyone struggling with understanding feelings and how they affect you not just mentally but physically to reach out to her. Coaching is definitely a different and in my opinion much more beneficial if traditional therapy is not helping like you want

I have to tell you.
I am thinking of me.
I feel powerful and happy.
Your book is soooo helpful
I love you
Thank you

Omg. Fantastic my friend
I really have been busy
going out of my comfort
zone. You have helped me
so much so far

What's working in your life right now?
(self-care, family, friends, relationships, work, etc.)

What is not working in your life right now?
(self-care, family, friends, relationships, work, etc.)

Owning our story and loving ourselves through that process is the bravest thing that we'll ever do."
~ Brené Brown, <u>Daring Greatly</u>

What do the words Fierce, Authentic, & Badass mean to you?
(When was the last time that you felt any or all of these?)

"Get Busy Living, Or Get Busy Dying."
~ Andy Dufresne (Tim Robbins)
in Shawshank Redemption

Are you playing small, feel like you're missing out on life, second guessing your decisions, feeling less than, or holding yourself back in some way?
(Describe what that feels like to you.)

> "Vulnerability is not winning or losing; it's having the courage to show up and be seen when we have no control over the outcome."
> ~ Brené Brown, Rising Strong

"Do not allow people to dim your shine because they are blinded. Tell them to put some sunglasses on.
~Lady Gaga

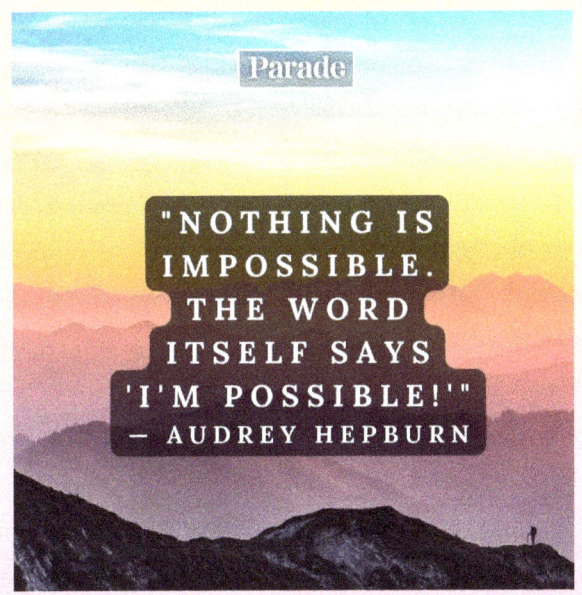

"NOTHING IS IMPOSSIBLE. THE WORD ITSELF SAYS 'I'M POSSIBLE!'"
— AUDREY HEPBURN

Describe your environment or surroundings.
Include your living space, the people you spend
time with, foods that you eat, places that you go.
(Do any of these bring you joy, peace, or love?)

"We either make ourselves miserable, or we make ourselves strong. The amount of work is the same."
~ Carlos Castaneda

What do you like about yourself? List at least 4-6 things you do like first and then what you don't.
(When was the last time that you were happy or proud of yourself?)

"When we work from a place that says, 'I'm enough' then we stop screaming and start listening, we're kinder and gentler to the people around us, and we're kinder and gentler to ourselves."

~ Brené Brown, The Power of Vulnerability TED Talk

How do you handle stress?
Do you eat everything in sight or nothing at all?
Bite your nails? Procrastinate until the deadline?
(Describe what you do during times of stress.)

"The bad news is time flies.
The good news is you're the pilot."
~ Michael Altshuler

How much sleep do you get? Do you allow yourself down time without guilt?
(How, if any, has this changed over time?)

"Without enough sleep, we all become tall two-year-olds."
~ Jojo Jensen

What does playing look like in your life right now? Do you have hobbies, go on vacation, spend time with kids or friends and family?
(If you don't currently play, list out why.)

"We don't stop playing because we grow old ... we grow old because we stop playing."
~ George Bernard Shaw

How often do you move your body?
What are you doing to move your body?
(Dance, swim, walk, etc. and if you don't currently get regular movement, list out why.)

"When we take care of ourselves first, we are in a much stronger place to take care of those we love."
~ Kate Hudson

"Vulnerability is the birthplace of love, belonging, joy, courage, empathy, and creativity. It is the source of hope, empathy, accountability, and authenticity. If we want greater clarity in our purpose or deeper and more meaningful spiritual lives, vulnerability is the path."
— Brené Brown

How do YOU feel about your body?
Like it? Meh? Disgust? Unsure?
Are you willing to learn to love and appreciate it? What comes up for you when you think about honoring your body?

Learning to love and be kind to ourselves is a lifelong journey."

~ Brené Brown, Daring Greatly: How the Courage to Be Vulnerable Transforms the Way We Live, Love, Parent, and Lead

Do you feel shame, guilt, or judgment?
Do you speak harshly to yourself?
(Is the "weight" you that holds you back Emotional or Physical?)

"Shame is the intensely painful feeling or experience of believing that we are flawed and therefore unworthy of love and belonging."
~ Brené Brown, Daring Greatly

List out any limiting beliefs you have.
This can be related to work, self-worth, good
health, money and abundance, or relationships.
(How do these differ from any self-doubts or fear you
may have?)

You make a choice:
Continue living your life feeling muddled in this abyss of
self=misunderstanding, or you find your identitiy
indepenedent of it. You draw your own box.
~Duchess Meghan

Describe how your life will feel once you have worked though your limiting beliefs to overcome the self-doubt and fear?
(Give yourself permission to go free with your answers.)

"I just want you to know that if you are out there and you are being really hard on yourself right now for something that has happened ... it's normal. That is what is going to happen to you in life. No one gets through unscathed. We are all going to have a few scratches on us. Please be kind to yourselves and stand up for yourself, please."
~Taylor Swift

How are the relationships in your life going?
Partner, parents, co-workers, friends, etc.
(Can you easily meet your needs before others?)

"Daring to set boundaries is about having the courage to love ourselves, even when we risk disappointing others.
~Brené Brown

"When you shut down emotion,
you're also affecting
your immune system,
your nervous system.
So the repression
of emotion,
which is a survival strategy,
then becomes a source
of physiological
illness later on."

– Gabor Maté

Let's get you to lean into your emotions, instead of shy away from them . . .

The
essence of
trauma is a
disconnect
from the self.

Therefore the
essence of healing
is not just uncovering
one's past, but
reconnecting with
oneself in the present.

Quote: Dr. Gabor Maté • Artist: Ileana Hunter

What methods have you already tried in your healing journey?
What worked vs what didn't?
(CBT, EMDR, Mindset work, etc.?)

"Success is not final, failure is not fatal: it is the courage to continue that counts."
~Winston Churchill

What does your self-care routine looks like?
(Does it include solo dinner dates, reading a good book, walk in nature, coloring or art, bubble bath, dance party, meditation, or journaling? If not, why?)

"Self-care is not self-indulgence, it is self-preservation."
~Audre Lorde

Quiz time!
Is my nervous system dysregulated?
(Complete the yes/no worksheet below)

1. I am constantly on edge, or overwhelmed. yes / no
2. I struggle with sleeping (insomnia, daytime fatigue, oversleeping, etc.). yes / no
3. I am frequently irritable, snippy, or find myself overreacting often. yes / no
4. I suffer from chronic pain or illnesses (not due to any injuries). yes / no
5. I have a history of unpleasant or traumatic childhood events, or chronic stress. yes / no
6. I have tried talk therapy, generic mindset work, or other cognitive options and still feel stuck.   yes / no
7. I have a difficult time staying focused, paying attention, or concentrating. yes / no
8. I suffer from appetite changes or specific cravings.   yes / no
9. I struggle to set boundaries, or compromise them in order to please others, while ignoring what I need. yes / no
10. I am highly sensitive to other people's emotions. yes / no
11. I tend to shut down or freeze during moments of stress. yes / no
12. I have a tendency to run from my scary emotions or problems. yes / no

If you answered yes to more than a few of these, you are most likely operating with a dysregulated nervous system. This awareness gives us a starting point to understanding where in your body you experience this dysregulation and how to begin to regulate your nervous system.

Do you know how your emotions show up in your body? Your body provides clues through sensations.
(Example: I am feeling angry and my jaw is clenched, my face feels warm)

Examples of what happens in Fight & Flight experiences:

Fight Body Experience
- Tension in muscles, hands, feet, and/or jaw.
- Increased heart rate.
- Impulse to kick, shout, bite, push, claw, strangle, etc.
- Holding of breath, or rapid shallow breathing.
- Blood flows away from vital organs, into extremities.
- Narrowing eyes, dilated pupils.
- Feeling aggression, anger or rage.
- Blunt pain response is compromised.
- Digestion, growth hormone production, & tissue repair are temporarily halted.
- Memory can be altered.

Flight Body Experiences
- High arousal in limbs (ie. trembling, shaking, twisting)
- Impulse to flee, back up, turn away, fly, not stop moving.
- Holding breath or rapid, shallow breathing (panting)
- Feeling a sense of urgency.
- Feelings of fear, anxiety or restlessness.
- Heart rate & blood pressure increases.
- Blood flows from vital organs to extremities.
- Digestion, growth hormone production & tissue repair are temporarily halted.
- Dilated pupils & darting eyes.
- Memory can be altered.

Examples of what happens in Freeze & Fawn experiences:

Freeze Body Experiences
- Paralysis, shut-down, frozen, still.
- Impulse to get small, hide, go away, disappear.
- Low oxygen state.
- Dissociation
- Shock, panic, overwhelm.
- Feeling stuck, in a certain part of the body.
- Feeling cold or numb.
- Decreased heart rate.
- Restricted breathing or holding of breath.
- Physical stiffness of heaviness of limbs.
- Blood flows away from limbs & into vital organs.
- Trouble thinking straight or making decisions.

Fawn Body Experiences
- Hardest to detect in the body, physically.
- Can mimic the 'freeze' response.
- Inability to say "no" or disagree.
- Shows up as people-pleasing or codependency.
- Over apologizing,
- Excessive concern over what others think.
- Fear of being seen or taking up too much space.
- Detachment from one's own discomfort or needs.
- Inability to recognize or regulate one's own emotions.
- Ignoring intuition.

What do you know about Body Positivity vs Body Neutrality? Do you believe that you can separate how your body provides for you from how you feel about it?

_____

_____

_____

_____

_____

_____

_____

_____

_____

_____

_____

_____

_____

_____

_____

_____

_____

_____

_____

Body Neutral Affirmations

1. My worth is not determined by a number.
2. I release all judgment about my body.
3. I am grateful for the ability to breathe, eat, see, walk, and hear.

What lights you up with joy?
How do you measure success in life?
(Consider other ways besides just money or saying you are happy. Take a minute to really think about these)

> "When we lose our tolerance for vulnerability,
> joy becomes foreboding."
> ~ Brené Brown

What are you grateful for in your life?
How do you show the Universe your gratitude?
(Do you journal, pay it forward to others, volunteer?)

"Gratitude makes sense of our past, brings peace for today, and creates a vision for tomorrow."
— Brené Brown, <u>Rising Strong</u>

PERFECTIONISM

The 20-ton shield we lug around hoping it protects us from experiencing judgment, shame, and blame, when all it really does is keep us from being seen.

And it's heavy AF.

Unlocking Us on Spotify
Summer Sister Series on *The Gifts of Imperfection* | Part 2 of 6

Notes & random thoughts ...

Notes & random thoughts ...

Notes & random thoughts ...

Notes & random thoughts ...

Notes & random thoughts ...

Notes & random thoughts ...

Notes & random thoughts ...

Gratitude Reflection
Write out what you are grateful for in completing this journal ...

YOU DID IT!!

You just tackled your BIG changes through a series of
very small, manageable concepts!

Growth is never-ending and there is always room
to expand your knowledge and continue to heal.

This is your permission slip to re-invent you!
You are worthy of feeling seen, heard, and loved.

Ready to go further on your journey to thrive instead of just survive?

Scan the QR code and find the link to a
FREEBIE 20-min Clarity Call
with me that will include *an easy, anytime
grounding exercise*!

https://checkya.com/fabapproach

"When we dare to drop the armor that protects us from feeling
vulnerable, we open ourselves to the possibility of love,
belonging, and joy."
— Brené Brown, <u>Daring Greatly</u>

www.ingramcontent.com/pod-product-compliance
Lightning Source LLC
Chambersburg PA
CBHW051219120626
46547CB00013B/1421